WHATEVER IS, IS BEST

Do not attempt to adopt the
style of any author. Unless
you can feel that you can be yourself
do not try to be anybody. A poor
original is better than a good
imitation in literature, if not in
other things.

Ella Wheeler Wilcox

Other books by

Blue Mountain Arts inc.

Come Into the Mountains, Dear Friend
by Susan Polis Schutz
I Want to Laugh, I Want to Cry
by Susan Polis Schutz
Peace Flows from the Sky
by Susan Pols Schutz

The Best Is Yet to Be
The International Grandmothers' Cookbook
Step to the Music You Hear, Vol. I
Step to the Music You Hear, Vol. II
The Desiderata of Happiness
The Language of Friendship
Poor Richard's Quotations
The Language of Love

Whatever Is, Is Best

A collection of poems
by Ella Wheeler Wilcox

Selected by Susan Polis Schutz
Designed by Dr. Stephen Schutz
With Illustrations by Leonard Matejcic

Blue
Mountain
Arts inc.

Boulder, Colorado

First Printing: June, 1975
Second Printing: August, 1975
Third Printing: November, 1975

Library of Congress Catalog Card Number: 75-13859
ISBN Number: 0-88396-011-7

Manufactured in the United States of America

Cover design and initial letter designs
are based on original editions of
Ella Wheeler Wilcox's books published
by W.B. Conkey Co., Chicago.

Layout by Roger Ben Wilson.
Editorial Assistance by Erin Russell.

Blue Mountain Arts inc.
P.O. Box 4549   Boulder, Colorado 80302

CONTENTS

INTRODUCTION

Ella Wheeler Wilcox is one of the few women poets to
become famous during her own lifetime. Such poems as
Solitude, Whatever Is—Is Best, Worth While, The Beautiful
Land of Nod, and The Winds of Fate, are so popular that they
are found in practically every anthology of American poetry.

Ella Wheeler Wilcox was born in 1850 to parents who
predicted even before she was born that she would be a
writer. At nine she wrote her first "novel", and at fourteen
her first essay and poem were published in national
magazines. By the time she was eighteen, between prizes and
magazine publications, she was earning a substantial
income. When asked by writers how she won the favor of
so many editors, she replied, "by sheer persistence . . . the
will in my own soul, and the patient and persistent effort of
mind and heart and hand . . . I pounded away at the doors
with my childish fist until they opened for me."

A collection of Ella Wheeler Wilcox's love poems entitled
"Poems of Passion" was refused by a publisher on moral
grounds. With its eventual publication by another publisher
in 1876, Ella Wheeler Wilcox found herself famous.

In 1884 she married Robert Wilcox, a manufacturer of
silver objects of art, and they lived in New York in the
winter and in Short Beach, Connecticut, in the summer. They
travelled a great deal, and among their friends were
prominent writers, artists and philosophers. During this
time Ella wrote many volumes of poetry and essays as well
as poems for magazines.

After her husband's death she became a spiritualist and a
theosophist. During World War I, on the strong belief
that her dead husband's spirit guided her actions, she toured
the American camps in France reading her poetry and
lecturing to soldiers. At nearly seventy, exhaustion from the
strain of this pilgrimage brought on a fatal illness. She
was taken from a nursing home in Bath, England, to
Connecticut where she soon died.

WHATEVER IS, IS BEST is a collection of some of Ella
Wheeler Wilcox's poems on faith, art and love. All of her

poems are spiritually and aesthetically meaningful. We hope that the well-deserved popularity of Ella Wheeler Wilcox will be renewed with this book.

—Susan Polis Schutz

"I know there are no errors,
  In the great Eternal plan,
And all things work together
  For the final good of man.
And I know when my soul speeds onward,
  In its grand Eternal quest,
I shall say as I look back earthward,
  Whatever is, is best."

Ella Wheeler Wilcox

WINDS OF FATE

"WHATEVER IS—IS BEST"

I know, as my life grows older,
   And mine eyes have clearer sight—
That under each rank Wrong, somewhere,
There lies the root of Right.
That each sorrow has its purpose—
   By the sorrowing oft unguessed,
But as sure as the Sun brings morning,
   Whatever is, is best.

I know that each sinful action,
   As sure as the night brings shade,
Is sometime, somewhere, punished,
   Tho' the hour be long delayed.
I know that the soul is aided
   Sometimes by the heart's unrest,
And to grow, means often to suffer—
   But whatever is, is best.

I know there are no errors,
   In the great Eternal plan,
And all things work together
   For the final good of man.

And I know when my soul speeds onward
   In the grand, Eternal quest,
I shall say, as I look back earthward,
   Whatever is, is best.

WORTH WHILE

It is easy enough to be pleasant,
   When life flows by like a song,
But the man worth while is one who will smile,
   When everything goes dead wrong.
For the test of the heart is trouble,
   And it always comes with the years,
And the smile that is worth the praises of earth,
   Is the smile that shines through tears.

It is easy enough to be prudent,
   When nothing tempts you to stray,
When without or within no voice of sin
   Is luring your soul away;
But it's only a negative virtue
   Until it is tried by fire,
And the life that is worth the honor on earth,
   Is the one that resists desire.

By the cynic, the sad, the fallen,
   Who had no strength for the strife,
The world's highway is cumbered to-day,
   They make up the sum of life.
But the virtue that conquers passion,
   And the sorrow that hides in a smile,
It is these that are worth the homage on earth,
   For we find them but once in a while.

WHICH ARE YOU?

There are two kinds of people on earth to-day;
Just two kinds of people, no more, I say.

Not the sinner and saint, for it's well understood,
The good are half bad, and the bad are half good.

Not the rich and the poor, for to rate a man's wealth,
You must first know the state of his conscience
and health.

Not the humble and proud, for in life's little span,
Who puts on vain airs, is not counted a man.

Not the happy and sad, for the swift flying years
Bring each man his laughter and each man his tears.

No; the two kinds of people on earth I mean,
Are the people who lift, and the people who lean.

Wherever you go, you will find the earth's masses,
Are always divided in just these two classes.

And oddly enough, you will find too, I ween,
There's only one lifter to twenty who lean.

In which class are you? Are you easing the load,
Of overtaxed lifters, who toil down the road?

Or are you a leaner, who lets others share
Your portion of labor, and worry and care?

PREACHING VS. PRACTICE

It is easy to sit in the sunshine
   And talk to the man in the shade;
It is easy to float in a well-trimmed boat,
   And point out the places to wade.

But once we pass into the shadows,
   We murmur and fret and frown,
And, our length from the bank, we shout for a plank,
   Or throw up our hands and go down.

It is easy to sit in your carriage,
   And counsel the man on foot,
But get down and walk, and you'll change your talk,
   As you feel the peg in your boot.

It is easy to tell the toiler
   How best he can carry his pack,
But no one can rate a burden's weight
   Until it has been on his back.

The up-curled mouth of pleasure,
   Can prate of sorrow's worth,
But give it a sip, and a wryer lip,
   Was never made on earth.

BE NOT CONTENT

Be not content, contentment means inaction,
   The growing soul aches on its upward quest;
   Satiety is twin to satisfaction—
All great achievements spring from life's unrest.

The tiny roots, deep in the dark mould hiding,
   Would never bless the earth with leaf and flower
Were not an inborn restlessness abiding
   In seed and germ, to stir them with its power.

Were man contented with his lot forever,
   He had not sought strange seas with sails unfurled,
And the vast wonder of our shores had never
   Dawned on the gaze of an admiring world.

Prize what is yours, but be not quite contented.
   There is a healthful restlessness of soul
By which a mighty purpose is augmented
   In urging men to reach a higher goal.

So when the restless impulse rises, driving
   Your calm content before it, do not grieve;
It is the upward reaching of the spirit
   Of the God in you to achieve, achieve.

SOLITUDE

Laugh, and the world laughs with you;
    Weep, and you weep alone.
For the sad old earth must borrow its mirth,
    But has trouble enough of its own.
Sing, and the hills will answer;
    Sigh, it is lost on the air,
The echoes bound to a joyful sound,
    But shrink from voicing care.

Rejoice, and men will seek you;
    Grieve, and they turn and go.
They want full measure of all your pleasure,
    But they do not need your woe.
Be glad, and your friends are many;
    Be sad, and you lose them all—
There are none to decline your nectar'd wine,
    But alone you must drink life's gall.

Feast, and your halls are crowded
    Fast, and the world goes by.
Succeed and give, and it helps you live,
    But no man can help you die.
There is room in the halls of pleasure
    For a large and lordly train,
But one by one we must all file on
    Through the narrow aisles of pain.

Whatever we intensely desire, must come to us. It is only a question of the force and constancy of our desire.

"IT MIGHT HAVE BEEN"

We will be what we could be. Do not say,
    "It might have been, had not or that, or this."
No fate can keep us from the chosen way;
    He only might, who is.

We will do what we could do. Do not dream
    Chance leaves a hero, all uncrowned to grieve.
I hold, all men are greatly what they seem;
    He does, who could achieve.

We will climb where we could climb. Tell me not
    Of adverse storms that kept thee from the height.
What eagle ever missed the peak he sought?
    He always climbs who might.

I do not like the phrase, "It might have been!"
    It lacks all force, and life's best truths perverts:
For I believe we have, and reach, and win,
    Whatever our deserts.

The world is kind, and there will be more hands held out ready to help you up than there were ready to beat you down; and, though you may be at the bottom of the ladder of health, morals and fortune, you may climb to the very top before another new year, if you only believe you can and resolve your will.

WILL

There is no chance, no destiny, no fate,
  Can circumvent or hinder or control
  The firm resolve of a determined soul.
Gifts count for nothing; will alone is great;
All things give way before it, soon or late.
  What obstacle can stay the mighty force
  Of the sea-seeking river in its course,
Or cause the ascending orb of day to wait?

Each well-born soul must win what it deserves.
Let the fool prate of luck. The fortunate
  Is he whose earnest purpose never swerves,
  Whose slightest action or inaction serves
The one great aim.
                Why, even Death stands still,
And waits an hour sometimes for such a will.

IT ALL WILL COME OUT RIGHT

Whatever is a cruel wrong,
  Whatever is unjust,
The honest years that speed along
  Will trample in the dust.
In restless youth I railed at fate
  With all my puny might,
But now I know if I but wait
  It all will come out right.

Though Vice may don the judge's gown
  And play the censor's part,
And Fact be cowed by Falsehood's frown
  And Nature ruled by art;
Though Labor toils through blinding tears
  And idle Wealth is might,
I know the honest, earnest years
  Will bring it all out right.

Though poor and loveless creeds may pass
  For pure religion's gold;
Though ignorance may rule the mass
  While truth meets glances cold,
I know a law complete, sublime,
  Controls us with its might,
And in God's own appointed time
  It all will come out right.

OPTIMISM

I'm no reformer; for I see more light
Than darkness in the world; mine eyes are quick
To catch the first dim radiance of the dawn,
And slow to note the cloud that threatens storm.
The fragrance and the beauty of the rose
Delight me so, slight thought I give its thorn;
And the sweet music of the lark's clear song,
Stays longer with me than the night hawk's cry.
And e'en in this great throe of pain called Life,
I find a rapture linked with each despair,
Well worth the price of Anguish. I detect
More good than evil in humanity.
Love lights more fires than hate extinguishes,
And men grow better as the world grows old.

TALK HAPPINESS

Talk happiness. The world is sad enough
　　Without your woes. No path is wholly rough;
Look for the places that are smooth and clear,
And speak of those, to rest the weary ear
Of Earth, so hurt by one continuous strain
Of human discontent and grief and pain.

Talk faith. The world is better off without
Your uttered ignorance and morbid doubt.
If you have faith in God, or man, or self,
Say so. If not, push back upon the shelf
Of silence all your thoughts, till faith shall come;
No one will ever grieve because your lips are dumb.

Talk health. The dreary, never-changing tale
Of mortal maladies is worn and stale.
You cannot charm, or interest, or please
By harping on that minor chord, disease.
Say you are well, or all is well with you,
And God shall hear your words and make them true.

THE WORLD'S NEED

So many gods, so many creeds,
 So many paths that wind and wind,
 While just the art of being kind,
Is all the sad world needs.

MY BELIEF

I believe that whatever is, is best, and the sufferings we are compelled to endure here are but the results of wrong methods of living, and thinking, in this or former lives, and are ripening experiences intended to force the soul into truer conditions.

I believe that we are evolved from lesser order of life through millions of centuries, and that humanity is the highest type yet obtained; that the world grows better and humanity more spiritual and intelligent constantly, and that we are all progressing towards divinity; that in time the earth will be inhabited by almost god-like beings, who shall analyze and discuss the remnants of humanity as we now discuss the chimpanzee.

THE WINDS OF FATE

One ship drives east and another drives west
With the self-same winds that blow;
    'Tis the set of the sails
    And not the gales
That tells them the way to go.

Like the winds of the sea are the winds of fate
As we voyage along through life;
    'Tis the set of the soul
    That decides its goal
And not the calm or the strife.

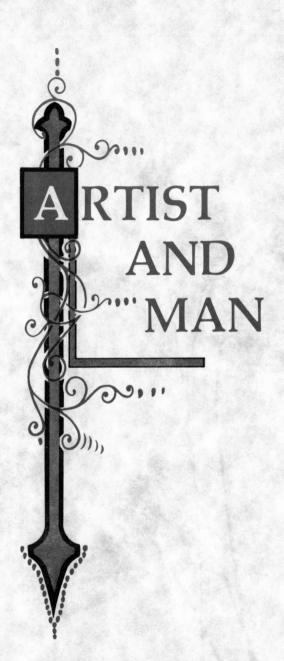

ARTIST
AND
MAN

ARTIST AND MAN

Make thy life better than thy work. Too oft
    Our artists spend their skill in rounding soft
        Fair curves upon their statues,
While the rough
And ragged edges of the unhewn stuff
In their own natures startle and offend
The eye of critic and the heart of friend.

If in thy too brief day thou must neglect
Thy labor of thy life, let men detect
Flaws in thy work! while their most searching gaze
Can fall on nothing which they may not praise
In thy well-chiseled character. The Man
Should not be shadowed by the Artisan!

Do not imagine because you feel strongly that you can write strongly. Feeling and expression are not twins. To the majority it is given to feel—to the few to express what the many feel.

Do not attempt to adopt the style of any author. Unless you can feel that you can be yourself do not try to be anybody. A poor original is better than a good imitation in literature, if not in other things.

ART AND HEART

Though critics may bow to art, and I am its own
  true lover,
It is not art, but heart, which wins the wide world over.

Though smooth be the heartless prayer, no ear in
  Heaven will mind it,
And the finest phrase falls dead, if there is no feeling
  behind it.

Though perfect the player's touch, little if any he
  sways us,
Unless we feel his heart throb through the music he
  plays us.

Though the poet may spend his life in skillfully
  rounding a measure,
Unless he writes from a full warm heart, he gives us
  little pleasure.

So is not the speech which tells, but the impulse which
  goes with the saying,
And it is not the words of the prayer, but the yearning
  back of the praying.

It is not the artist's skill, which into our soul comes
    stealing
With a joy that is almost pain, but it is the player's
    feeling.

And it is not the poet's song, though sweeter than
    sweet bells chiming.
Which thrills us through and through, but the heart
    which beats under the rhyming.

And therefore I say again, though I am art's own
    true lover,
That it is not art, but heart, which wins the wide
    world over.

LINES FROM "MAURINE"

I'd rather have my verses win
   A place in common peoples' hearts,
Who, toiling through the strife and din
   Of life's great thoroughfares, and marts,

May read some line my hand has penned;
   Some simple verse, not fine, or grand,
   But what their hearts can understand
And hold me henceforth as a friend—

I'd rather win such quiet fame
   Than by some fine thought, polished so
   But those of learned minds would know,
   Just what the meaning of my song—
To have the critics sound my name
   In high-flown praises, loud and long.

I sing not for the critic's ear,
But for the masses. If they hear,
Despite the turmoil, noise and strife
Some least low note that gladdens life,
I shall be wholly satisfied,
Though critics to the end deride.

THE TECHNIQUE OF IMMORTALITY

There hangs a picture on my wall;
  Three leafless trees; dead woods beyond;
Brown grasses and a marshy pond;
And over all
An amber sunset of late fall.

Too frail the artist heart to cope
With all the stern demands of fame.
He passed before he won a name,
Or gained his hope,
To realms where dreams have larger scope.

Yet in the modest little square
Of canvas, that I daily see,
He left a legacy to me
Of something rare;
Far more than what is painted there.

For tree and grass and sunset sky
Hold subtler qualities than art.
It is the painter's pulsing heart
That seems to cry,
"I loved these things—they cannot die."

And so they live; to stir and move
Each gazer's soul; because they speak
Of something mightier than technique.
They live to prove
The immortality of love.

They speak this message day by day;
"Love, love your work, or small or great;
Love, love, and leave the rest to fate.
For love will stay
When all things else have passed away."

NEVER MIND

Whatever your work and whatever its worth,
   No matter how strong or clever,
Some one will sneer if you pause to hear
   And scoff at your best endeavor,
For the target art has a broad expanse,
   And wherever you chance to hit it,
Though close be your aim to the bullseye fame,
   There are those who will never admit it.

Though the house applauds while the artist plays
   And a smiling world adores him,
Somebody is there with an ennuied air
   To say that the acting bores him.
For the tower of art has a lofty spire
   With many a stair and landing,
And those who climb seem small oft time
   To one at the bottom standing.

So work along in your chosen niche
   With a steady purpose to nerve you;
Let nothing men say who pass your way
   Relax your courage or swerve you.
The idle will flock by the Temple of Art
   For just the pleasure of gazing,
But climb to the top and do not stop
   Though they may not all be praising.

WHAT
LOVE
IS

WHAT LOVE IS

Love is the essence of every existing thing: the root of life!

It is the all creative spark, the vital force of the universe. There is power to achieve in the mere utterance of the word—Love. I think God said: "I love the earth," and lo! the earth sprang into being. Love is the natural element of all things. The illimitable oceans of space are composed of the waters of Love. Whoever loves most widely and warmly is most in harmony with the universe. Love is the key to success. To love your work is to excel in it. To love observingly and nobly any worthy object or aim is to eventually obtain and attain it.

WE TWO

We two make home of any place we go;
    We two find joy in any kind of weather;
Or if the earth is clothed in bloom or snow,
If Summer days invite or bleak winds blow,
    What matters it if we two are together?
    We two, we two, we make our world, our weather.

We two make banquets of the plainest fare;
    In every cup we find the thrill of pleasure;
We hide with wreaths the furrowed brow of care
And win to smiles the set lips of despair.
    For us life always moves with lilting measure;
    We two, we two, we make our world, our pleasure.

We two find youth renewed with every dawn;
    Each day holds something of an unknown glory.
We waste no thought on grief or pleasure gone;
Tricked out like Hope, Time leads us on and on,
    And thrums upon his harp new song or story.
    We two, we two, we find the paths of glory.

We two make heaven here on this little earth;
    We do not need to wait for realms eternal.
We know the use of tears, know sorrow's worth,
And pain for us is always love's rebirth.
    Our paths lead closely by the paths supernal;
    We two, we two, we live in love eternal.

FRIENDSHIP

Dear friend, I pray thee, if thou wouldst
    be proving
    Thy strong regard for me,
Make me no vows. Lip-service is not loving;
    Let thy faith speak for thee.

Swear not to me that nothing can divide us—
    So little such oaths mean.
But when distrust and envy creep beside us
    Let them not come between.

Say not to me the depths of thy devotion
    Are deeper than the sea;
But watch, lest doubt or some unkind emotion
    Embitter them for me.

Vow not to love me ever and forever,
    Words are such idle things;
But when we differ in opinions, never
    Hurt me by little stings.

I'm sick of words: they are so lightly spoken,
    And spoken, are but air.
I'd rather feel thy trust in me unbroken
    Than list thy words so fair.

If all the little proofs of trust are heeded,
    If thou art always kind,
No sacrifice, no promise will be needed
    To satisfy my mind.

UPON THE SAND

All love that has not friendship for its base,
    Is like a mansion built upon the sand.
  Though brave its walls as any in the land,
And its tall turrets lift their heads in grace;
Though skillful and accomplished artists trace
  Most beautiful designs on every hand,
  And gleaming statues in dim niches stand,
And fountains play in some flow'r-hidden place:

Yet, when from the frowning east a sudden gust
  Of adverse fate is blown, or sad rains fall
  Day in, day out, against its yielding wall,
Lo! the fair structure crumbles to the dust.
Love, to endure life's sorrow and earth's woe,
Needs friendship's solid masonwork below.

"ADVICE"

I must do as you do? Your way I own
 Is a very good way. And still,
There are sometimes two straight roads to a town,
 One over, one under the hill.

You are treading the safe and the well-worn way,
 That the prudent choose each time;
And you think me reckless and rash to-day,
 Because I prefer to climb.

Your path is the right one, and so is mine.
 We are not like peas in a pod,
Compelled to lie in a certain line,
 Or else be scattered abroad.

'T were a dull old world, methinks, my friend,
 If we all went just one way;
Yet our paths will meet no doubt at the end,
 Though they lead apart to-day.

You like the shade, and I like the sun;
 You like an even pace,
I like to mix with the crowd and run,
 And then rest after the race.

I like danger, and storm and strife,
    You like a peaceful time;
I like the passion and surge of life,
    You like its gentle rhyme.

You like buttercups, dewy sweet,
    And crocuses, framed in snow;
I like roses, born of the heat,
    And the red carnation's glow.

I must live my life, not yours, my friend,
    For so it was written down;
We must follow our given paths to the end,
    But I trust we shall meet—in town.

AN ANSWER

If all the year was summertime,
   And all the aim of life
  Was just to lilt on like a rhyme—
  Then I would be your wife.

If all the days were August days,
   And crowned with golden weather,
How happy then through green-clad ways
   We two could stray together!

If all the nights were moonlit nights,
   And we had naught to do
But just to sit and plan delights,
   Then I would wed with you.

If life was all a summer fete,
   Its soberest pace the "glide,"
Then I would choose you for my mate,
   And keep you at my side.

But winter makes full half the year,
    And labor half of life,
And all the laughter and good cheer
    Give place to wearing strife.
Days will grow cold, and moons wax old,
    And then a heart that's true
Is better far than grace or gold—
    And so my love, adieu!
    I cannot wed with you.

SURRENDER

Love, when we met, 'twas like two planets meeting.
   Strange chaos followed; body, soul, and heart
Seemed shaken, thrilled, and startled by that greeting.
   Old ties, old dreams, old aims, all torn apart
And wrenched away, left nothing there the while
   But the great shining glory of your smile.

I knew no past; 'twas all a blurred, bleak waste;
   I asked no future; 'twas a blinding glare.
I only saw the present: as men taste
   Some stimulating wine, and lose all care,
I tasted Love's elixir, and I seemed
   Dwelling in some strange land, like one who dreamed.

It was a godlike separate existence;
   Our world was set apart in some fair clime.
I had no will, no purpose, no resistance;
   I only knew I loved you for all time.
The earth seemed something foreign and afar,
   And we two, sovereigns dwelling in a star!

It is so sad, so strange, I almost doubt
   That all those years could be, before we met.
Do you not wish that we could blot them out?
   Obliterate them wholly, and forget
That we had any part in life until
   We clasped each other with Love's rapture thrill?

My being trembled to its very centre
   At that first kiss. Cold Reason stood aside
With folded arms to let a grand Love enter
   In my Soul's secret chamber to abide.
Its great High Priest, my first Love and my last,
   There on its altar I consumed my past.

And all my life I lay upon its shrine
   The best emotions of my heart and brain,
Whatever gifts and graces may be mine;
   No secret thought, no memory I retain,
But give them all for dear Love's precious sake;
   Complete surrender of the whole I make.

AN UNFAITHFUL WIFE TO HER HUSBAND

Branded and blackened by my own misdeeds
I stand before you; not as one who pleads
For mercy or forgiveness, but as one,
After a wrong is done,
Who seeks the why and wherefore.
                    Go with me
Back to those early years of love, and see
Just where our paths diverged. You must recall
Your wild pursuit of me, outstripping all
Competitors and rivals, till at last
You bound me sure and fast
With vow and ring.
I was the central thing
In all the Universe for you just then.
Just then for me, there were no other men.
I cared
Only for tasks and pleasures that you shared.
Such happy, happy days. You wearied first.
I will not say you wearied, but a thirst
For conquest and achievement in man's realm
Left love's barque with no pilot at the helm.
The money madness, and the keen desire
To outstrip others, set your heart on fire.
Into the growing conflagration went
Romance and sentiment.
Abroad you were a man of parts and power—
Your double dower
Of brawn and brains gave you a leader's place;
At home you were dull, tired, and commonplace.
You housed me, fed me, clothed me; you were kind;
But oh, so blind, so blind.
You could not, would not, see my woman's need
Of small attentions; and you gave no heed
When I complained of loneliness; you said
"A man must think about his daily bread
And not waste time in empty social life—
He leaves that sort of duty to his wife

And pays her bills, and lets her have her way,
And feels she should be satisfied."
                    Each day
Our lives that had been one life at the start,
Farther and farther seemed to drift apart.
Dead was the old romance of man and maid.
Your talk was all of politics or trade.
Your work, your club, the mad pursuit of gold
Absorbed your thoughts. Your duty kiss fell cold
Upon my lips. Life lost its zest, its thrill,
                    Until
One fateful day when earth seemed very dull
It suddenly grew bright and beautiful.
I spoke a little, and he listened much;
There was attention in his eyes, and such
A note of comradeship in his low tone,
I felt no more alone.
There was a kindly interest in his air;
He spoke about the way I dressed my hair.
And praised the gown I wore.
It seemed a thousand, thousand years and more
Since I had been so noticed. Had mine ear
Been used to compliments year after year,
If I had heard you speak
As this man spoke, I had not been so weak.
The innocent beginning
Of all my sinning
Was just the woman's craving to be brought
Into the inner shrine of some man's thought.
You held me there, as sweetheart and as bride;
And then as wife, you left me far outside.
So far, so far, you could not hear me call;
You might, you should, have saved me from my fall.
I was not bad, just lonely, that was all.

A man should offer something to replace
The sweet adventure of the lover's chase
Which ends with marriage, Love's neglected laws
Pave pathways for the "Statutory Cause."

LOVE AND FRIENDSHIP

Love stands alone in the solar system of the affections like the sun, unmated and incomparable. From it all the other emotions derive their worth, yet they must not expect to imitate its light, warmth, or power.

Our friendships are the stars next in magnitude to the orb of light. There can be but one true love, as there is but one sun visible to the earth. But there may be as many orders of friendship as there are varieties of stars in the firmament, though few, to be sure, of the first magnitude.

Those who belong to each other spiritually, will find each other and dwell together through eternities of love.

❧

He who loves greatly hates feebly. All strong emotions proceed from and derive their strength from Love. If Love uses his own force there is nothing left for Hate.

God, what a world if men in street and mart
    Felt that same kinship of the human heart
Which makes them, in the face of fire and flood
Rise to the meaning of true brotherhood.

IMPATIENCE

How can I wait until you come to me?
  The once fleet mornings linger by the way;
Their sunny smiles touched with malicious glee
  At my unrest, they seem to pause, and play
  Like truant children, while I sigh and say,
    How can I wait?

How can I wait? Of old, the rapid hours
  Refused to pause or loiter with me long;
But now they idly fill their hands with flowers,
  And make no haste, but slowly stroll among
  The summer blooms, not heeding my one song,
    How can I wait?

How can I wait? The nights alone are kind;
  They reach forth to a future day, and bring
Sweet dreams of you to people all my mind;
  And time speeds by on light and airy wing.
  I feast upon your face, I no more sing,
    How can I wait?

How can I wait? The morning breaks the spell
 A pitying night has flung upon my soul.
You are not near me, and I know full well
 My heart has need of patience and control;
 Before we meet, hours, days and weeks must roll.
  How can I wait?

How can I wait? Oh, love, how can I wait
 Until the sunlight of your eyes shall shine
Upon my world that seems so desolate?
 Until your hand-clasp warms my blood like wine;
 Until you come again, oh, Love of mine,
  How can I wait?

LOVE MUCH

Love much. Earth has enough of bitter in it.
  Cast sweets into its cup whene'er you can:
No heart so hard, but love at last may win it.
  Love is the grand primeval cause of man.
  All hate is foreign to the first great plan.

Love much. Your heart will be led out to slaughter,
  On alters built of envy and deceit.
Love on, love on! 'tis bread upon the water;
  It shall be cast in loaves yet at your feet,
  Unleavened manna, most divinely sweet.

Love much. Your faith will be dethroned and shaken,
  Your trust betrayed by many a fair, false lure.
Remount your faith, and let new trusts awaken.
  Though clouds obscure them, yet the stars are pure;
  Love is a vital force and must endure.

Love much. Men's souls contract with cold suspicion:
  Shine on them with warm love, and they expand.
'Tis love, not creeds, that from a low condition
  Leads mankind up to heights supreme and grand.
  Oh, that the world could see and understand!

Love much. There is no waste in freely giving;
  More blessed is it, even, than to receive.
He who loves much, alone finds life worth living,
  Love on, through doubt and darkness; and believe
  There is no thing which Love may not achieve.

You may as well talk of hiding the glory of the sunrise from the earth, as the fervor of a great passion from the object which inspired it.

❧

Think Love, although you speak it not, it gives the world more light.

I LOVE YOU

I love your lips when they're wet with wine
  And red with a wild desire;
I love your eyes when the lovelight lies
  Lit with a passionate fire.
I love your arms when the warm white flesh
  Touches mine in a fond embrace;
I love your hair when the strands enmesh
  Your kisses against my face.

Not for me the cold, calm kiss
  Of a virgin's bloodless love;
Not for me the saint's white bliss,
  Nor the heart of a spotless dove.
But give me the love that so freely gives
  And laughs at the whole world's blame,
With your body so young and warm in my arms,
  It sets my poor heart aflame.

So kiss me sweet with your warm wet mouth,
  Still fragrant with ruby wine,
And say with a fervor born of the South
  That your body and soul are mine.
Clasp me close in your warm young arms,
  While the pale stars shine above,
And we'll live our whole young lives away
  In the joys of a living love.

BLEAK WEATHER

Dear Love, where the red lilies blossomed and grew
  The white snows are falling;
And all through the woods where I wandered with you
  The loud winds are calling;
And the robin that piped to us, tune upon tune,
  'Neath the oak, you remember,
O'er hilltop and forest has followed the June
  And left us December.

He has left like a friend who is true in the sun
  And false in the shadows;
He has found new delights in the land where he's gone,
  Greener woodlands and meadows.
Let him go! what care we? let the snow shroud the lea,
  Let it drift on the heather;
We can sing through it all: I have you, you have me,
  And we'll laugh at the weather.

The old year may die and a new year be born
  That is bleaker and colder:
It cannot dismay us; we dare it, we scorn,
  For our love makes us bolder.
Ah, Robin! sing loud on your far distant lea,
  You friend in fair weather!
But here is a song sung that's fuller of glee
  By two warm hearts together.

THE BEAUTIFUL LAND OF NOD

Come, cuddle your head on my shoulder, dear,
   Your head like the golden-rod,
  And we will go sailing away from here
  To the beautiful Land of Nod.
Away from life's hurry, and flurry, and worry,
   Away from earth's shadows and gloom,
To a world of fair weather we'll float off together
   Where roses are always in bloom.

Just shut up your eyes, and fold your hands,
   Your hands like the leaves of a rose,
And we will go sailing to those fair lands
   That never an atlas shows.
On the North and the West they are bounded by rest,
   On the South and the East, by dreams;
'Tis the country ideal, where nothing is real,
   But everything only seems.

Just drop down the curtains of your dear eyes,
  Those eyes like a bright blue-bell,
And we will sail out under starlit skies,
  To the land where the fairies dwell.
Down the river of sleep, our barque shall sweep,
  Till it reaches that mystical Isle
Which no man hath seen, but where all have been,
  And there we will pause awhile.
I will croon you a song as we float along,
  To that shore that is blessed of God,
Then ho! for that fair land, we're off for that rare land,
  That beautiful Land of Nod.